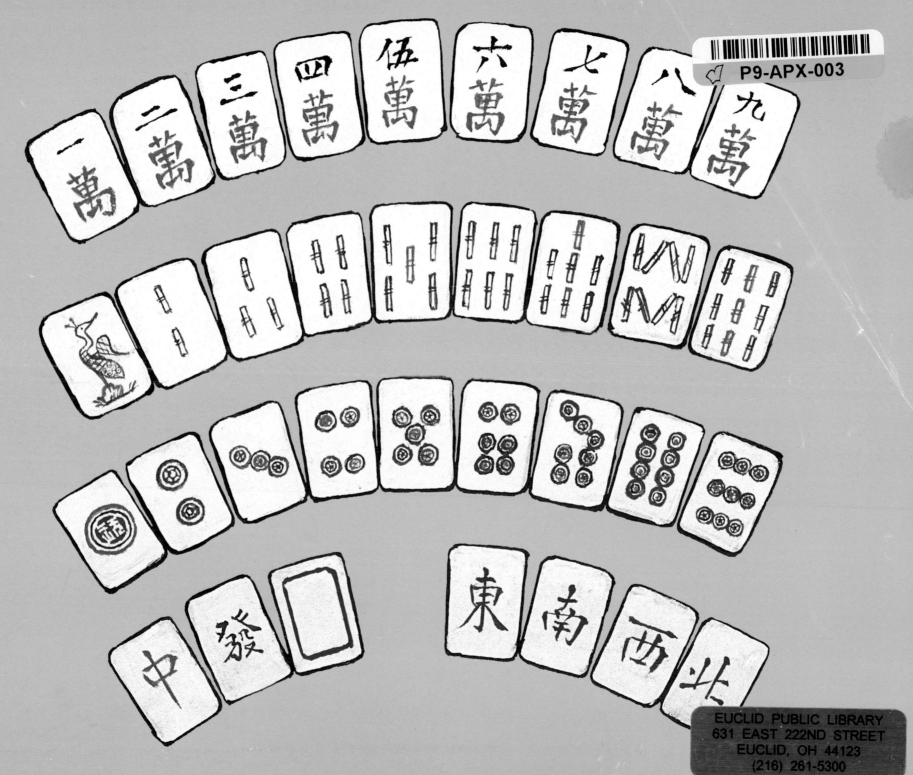

MAHJONG

ALL DAY LONG

STORY BY
Ginnie Lo

ILLUSTRATIONS BY
Beth Lo

Walker & Company ❧ New York

姐姐
JieJie
(Big Sister)

爸爸
BaBa
(Daddy)

媽媽
MaMa
(Mommy)

弟弟
DiDi
(Little Brother)

For Daddy and Mommy

Thanks to Mommy (Kiahsuang Shen Lo) for the calligraphy, David for the inspired editing,
Paul, Roo, Maika, and Tai for your love and support, and the Yangs and Shus for our wonderful mahjong memories.

Special thanks to Dr. Jean Yuanpeng Wu, Department of East Asian Languages and Literatures, University of Oregon.

Text copyright © 2005 by Virginia Mary Lo
Illustrations copyright © 2005 by Elizabeth Ann Lo

First published in the United States of America in 2005 by Walker Publishing Company, Inc.

Published simultaneously in Canada by Fitzhenry and Whiteside, Markham, Ontario L3R 4T8

For information about permission to reproduce selections from
this book, write to Permissions, Walker & Company, 104 Fifth Avenue, New York, New York 10011.

Library of Congress Cataloging-in-Publication Data
Lo, Ginnie.
Mahjong all day long / story by Ginnie Lo ; illustrations by Beth Lo.
p. cm.
ISBN 0-8027-8941-2 — ISBN 0-8027-8942-0
1. Mah jong—Juvenile literature. I. Lo, Beth. II. Title.
GV1299.M3L64 2005
795.34—dc22
2004049478

The artist used underglazes and stains on handmade porcelain plates to create the illustrations for this book.
Plates photographed by Chris Autio.

Book design by Victoria Allen

Visit Walker & Company's Web site at www.walkeryoungreaders.com

Printed in Hong Kong

2 4 6 8 10 9 7 5 3 1

And all night long.

和了

"Hu Le!" (I win!)

We hear the clicking of mahjong tiles morning, noon, and night

"Peng" (three of a kind)   "Chi" (three in a row)   Do you want this tile?

Uncle T. T. sings Chinese opera
while he plays.

Tape recorder

Sounds terrible!

Auntie Helen nibbles on watermelon seeds.

Tasty!

MaMa serves everyone
Long Jing tea.

不 要 發 瘋

Don't act crazy.

And BaBa lets me watch
from his lap.

Games

Sometimes DiDi gets to

roll the dice.

揺

Shake

When they finally stop playing,
we help pack the mahjong tiles
back into the trays—just so—
otherwise they won't all fit.

Working

We used to think mahjong tiles were for building tower bridges and long, winding snakes . . .

Working

Playing

or for learning how to
count in Chinese.

Now we're grown
and have children of our own.

1   2   3   4   5   6   7   8   9   10

We know all the mahjong rules and high-scoring combinations.

The Double Dragon   17 points   The 18 Buddhist Disciples   32 points

These days Uncle T. T. sings a little out of tune, and Auntie Helen can't crack the watermelon seeds anymore. But MaMa serves as much tea as ever.

愛

Hot!

And BaBa teaches his
grandchildren how to play.

不要碰

Don't touch!

Three generations happily playing mahjong all day long.

Mahjong

Mahjong 1960s

Mahjong 2000s

Some people believe that the game of mahjong was invented in ancient times by a lonely Chinese princess who was not allowed to leave the emperor's court. Others claim that the philosopher Confucius played mahjong over two thousand years ago. However, mahjong as it is played today dates back only two hundred years ago to a set-forming card game that was popular on the eastern coast of China.

The word *mahjong* (often spelled *mah-jongg*) means "hemp bird" or "sparrow," perhaps because the clicking of the tiles resembles the twittering of a sparrow, or because getting the winning tile is as difficult as catching a sparrow, the Chinese bird of cleverness. The delicate sparrow pattern is carved on four tiles in every mahjong set.

Mahjong is a four-person game, similar to gin rummy but played with tiles instead of cards. Altogether there are 136 or 144 tiles and each player tries to develop a winning hand of 14 to 16 tiles. There are many possible winning patterns of tiles, some worth a lot of points, others worth only one or two points.

Because it is very hard to win with a high-scoring hand, mahjong has been called "the game of one hundred intelligences."

Mahjong was brought over to the United States from Shanghai in the 1920s by an American businessman. During the following decade, it became wildly popular. Sets made of bone, ivory, bamboo, wood, and paper were imported in huge numbers from China. Soon American companies began manufacturing mahjong sets, some working twenty-four hours a day to keep up with the demand. After the 1930s the popularity of mahjong declined, but it has always had loyal fans from all cultures and of all ages. Recently, perhaps because many people have traveled to China, a new wave of interest in mahjong has arisen.

Some families play mahjong seriously, and talking is not allowed so that the players can concentrate. Our family plays for fun, so the room is full of chatter and laughter, along with delicious Chinese snacks served with steaming hot glasses of green tea.

We hope you enjoyed our story, and maybe some day you'll have a chance to play mahjong—for as long as you'd like.

If you'd like to learn to play mahjong, you might try one of the following books:

Kanai, Shozo, and Margaret Farrell. *Mah Jong for Beginners*. Boston: Tuttle, 1989.

Kohnen, Dieter. *Mah-Jongg: Basic Rules & Strategies*. New York: Sterling, 1998.

Lo, Amy. *The Book of Mahjong: An Illustrated Guide*. Boston: Tuttle, 2001.

McKeithan, Nancy. *Let's Play Mah Jong*. Victoria, BC, Canada: Trafford, 2002.

Pritchard, David. *Teach Yourself Mahjong*. Chicago: McGraw-Hill/Contemporary, 2001.

Strauser, Kitty. *Mah Jong, Anyone? A Manual of Modern Play*. Boston: Tuttle, 2002.

Thompson, Patricia A. *The Game of Mah Jong Illustrated*. East Roseville, NSW: Simon & Schuster Australia, 1999.

————. *The Mah Jong Player's Companion*. East Roseville, NSW: Simon & Schuster Australia, 2001.

Tjoa, Tong Seng. *Mah Jong Fun: A Handbook of Classic Fundamentals of Mah Jong*. New York: Vantage Press, 2003.

Whitney, Eleanor Noss. *A Mah Jong Handbook: How to Play, Score, and Win the Modern Game*. Boston: Tuttle, 1965.

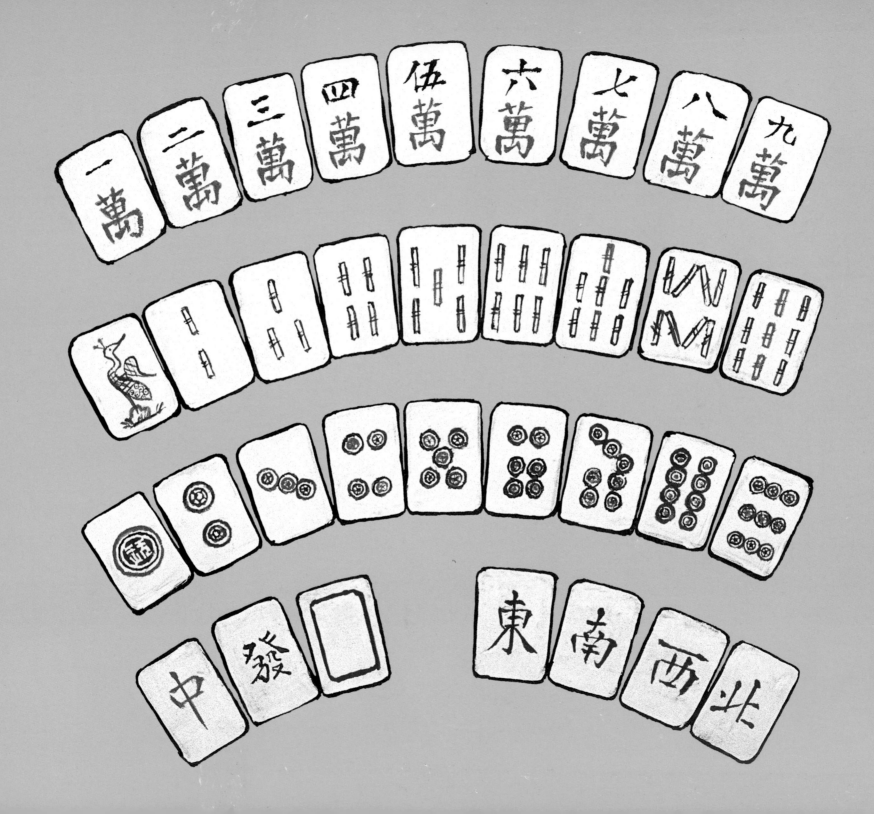